I Hear Thunder

An anthology of counting and action rhymes
Written and compiled by David Orme
Illustrated by Wendy Sinclair

Contents

Collins Educational

Keep fit

This is the way we stretch our arms,
Stretch our arms, stretch our arms.
This is the way we stretch our arms,
We'll all be fit in the morning!

This is the way we touch our toes,
Touch our toes, touch our toes.
This is the way we touch our toes,
We'll all be fit in the morning!

This is the way we swing our hips,
Swing our hips, swing our hips.
This is the way we swing our hips,
We'll all be fit in the morning!

This is the way we jump and clap,
Jump and clap, jump and clap.
This is the way we jump and clap,
We'll all be fit in the morning!

This is the way we sit and rest,
Sit and rest, sit and rest.
This is the way we sit and rest,
We're all tired out in the morning!

I hear thunder

I hear thunder, I hear thunder.
Hark, don't you? Hark, don't you?
Pitter-patter raindrops,
Pitter-patter raindrops,
I'm wet through.
So are you!

I see blue skies, I see blue skies,
Way up high, way up high.
Hurry up the sunshine,
Hurry up the sunshine,
We'll soon dry.
We'll soon dry!

Incy Wincy Spider

Incy Wincy Spider climbing
up the spout,
Down come the raindrops to wash
poor Incy out.
Out comes the sun to dry up
all the rain,
And Incy Wincy Spider climbs
the spout again.

Wet play

Wet play! Wet play!
What are we going
to do today?

Read my book,
Read my book.
That's what I shall do!

Wet play! Wet play!
What are we going
to do today?

Draw and paint,
Draw and paint.
That's what I shall do!

Wet play! Wet play!
What are we going
to do today?

Build up bricks,
Build up bricks.
That's what I shall do!

Wet play! Wet play!
What are we going
to do today?

Sit and sulk,
Sit and sulk.
That's what I shall do!

One, two, three, four, five

One, two, three, four, five,
Once I caught a fish alive.

Six, seven, eight, nine, ten,
Then I let it go again.

Why did you let it go?
Because it bit my finger so!

Which finger did it bite?
This little finger on my right!